Best Dogs & P... Kids Boo...

Billy Grinslott & Kinsey Marie Books
ISBN - 9781957881959

French Bulldogs are one of the 5 most popular breeds, and the most popular toy dog breed in America.

They're small enough to be great playmates for kids. These toy dogs, have a sturdy frame that fares well with kids of all ages

The English Cocker Spaniel. These dogs have a personality that's wonderful to be around.

There are few dogs as kind, sweet and loving as the English Cocker Spaniel. Because of their calm and silent nature, they get along with all kids. They Are the Smallest Sporting Breed of all dogs.

The Labrador Retriever is America's most popular dog. There are many types of colors for Labrador retrievers. Black, yellow, chocolate, red and white. Labradors get excited when playing with kids, and will need training. But at the core, the Labrador is a good-natured and kind dog. While their friendliness disqualifies them from being guard dogs, they'll always treat your kids right and are great for playtime.

Labrador Retrievers love the water. Labradors have webbed toes and are great swimmers. Their coat has two layers, a short, thick topcoat and a relatively water-resistant undercoat. They love to play in the water. They are the most used breed for guide dogs. They are among the world's most versatile workers, Labs can do almost anything and are fun dogs.

The flat coated retriever is friendly and sociable with everyone. There's not a single person these loving dogs can't befriend and with kids, they're superb. These dogs are sweet and dependable and will always have your children's back. These dogs are highly intelligent and active, and they tend to retain their puppy-like behaviors even well into adulthood. Flat-Coats are very intelligent, responsive, and eager to please, so they are generally easy to train. They always have a positive outlook on life. They will always make you laugh.

The Curly-Coated Retriever checks all the boxes when looking for the perfect family dog. They are friendly yet clever dogs that love to have fun. They have a typical retriever temperament that all kids can fall in love with. Curly-Coated Retrievers have straight hair on their face, but curly hair on their body. They love to play in the water like most labs. Curlies only need minimal grooming.

The Border Terrier was specifically bred to be kind and sweet. The Border Terrier has a pack-dog mentality. They see kids, as fellow companions of the pack or family. Border terriers are affectionate dogs with a lot of personality. Border Terriers love exploring outdoors and make fine childhood playmates. They love to play and get a lot of exercise.

The Schipperke is all about love and devotion. They simply adore kids. The Schipperke will get along with everyone, even cats and other dogs. The Schipperke is sometimes referred to as the little black fox. Standing no higher than 13 inches, Schipperkes are small dogs. The only downside is they like to bark, they can be noisey.

The Brittany Spaniel is known for their happy-go-lucky temperaments, which can make them some of the best playmates for older kids and adults. They can be sensitive, but they're gentle dogs. Brittany's are true companions and are devoted to their family. They're considered among the most versatile of bird dogs. Brittany's have a high energy level and love to play or exercise. Given enough exercise, they're doting, patient, and gentle in the home.

The Irish Setter will always greet you with a bright smile and tail wags. They're friendly and enthusiastic dogs with a soft spot for children. Irish Setters have a cheerful energy that's contagious and will shower kids with affection. They love to be around kids. The Irish setter loves to run and exercise, which is perfect for active kids.

The Cane Corso is a larger dog. When properly socialized and trained, the Cane Corso is the perfect addition to a house with kids. Cane Corso's are typically calm and mild-mannered around small children, though they love to play around with older kids. Socialization and training are required with these dogs, because they are big and sometimes will show their brute size.

Chesapeake Bay Retrievers typically enjoy the company of children and have a mild temperament. The Chesapeake has a watchful eye that's ideal for those needing a second pair of eyes on the little ones. Chesapeake Bay Retrievers have webbed feet and love to play in the water. Hiking, running, hunting, and swimming are what they love to do. The Chesapeake is a High-Energy Dog Breed and are great for active kids.

The Newfoundland is a gentle giant suited for children of all ages. The Newfoundland is always patient, gentle and friendly when it comes to the handling of small kids. They have a protective side to them, but they're typically not possessive or territorial. They are amazing swimmers and make great water rescue dogs. Newfoundland puppies love to eat. They can grow larger than people.

Even though Bernese Mountain Dogs are giant canines, they tend to do very well with children no matter what age. The best child-friendly trait of the Bernese is their patience. Bernese Mountains Dogs are handsome, even majestic. This is a cold-weather dog, they like living in cooler areas. A Bernese Mountain Dog will be your best friend. Bernese mountain dogs have a long coat and shed all year. Bernese mountain dogs do well in dog sports.

Boston Terriers are patient, sweet, friendly, and low maintenance. Just put them in the hands of kids, and they'll fall in love in no time. What makes the Boston Terrier ideal for children is their size. They're relatively small dogs, so they won't likely knock over a small child. They are highly intelligent and easy to train. They like a good amount of exercise, especially if it involves playtime with humans. They can provide endless entertainment with their silly antics and they like to have fun.

The Golden Retriever is undeniably one of America's favorite dogs. Golden Retrievers are intelligent, good-natured, sweet and reliable pets. They have all the qualities of a kid-friendly dog. Golden Retrievers need lots of exercise. Golden Retrievers make top-notch therapy dogs. Golden Retrievers often stay young at heart. Golden Retrievers love to eat. When carrying objects, they're known for their soft mouths.

The Cavalier King Charles Spaniel is one of the best toy companions in the world. Known for being playful and charming, they connect with children with little ease. They make great therapy dogs. They're lapdogs, but they're also sporting dogs, they are natural athletes.

English Springer Spaniels are great with children and other pets of the family. They are affectionate and sweet with kids. They're always eager to join kids in some family-friendly activities. Springer Spaniels have a good sense of humor and they love to have fun. English Springer Spaniels have a great nose for smelling things and are regularly used by the police as search dogs.

The Great Pyrenees is a wonderful large companion to have in a household with children. They are calm and gentle dogs, who knows how to behave around kids. The best part is the loyalty that they develop towards all members of the family. They were bred to be guard dogs. They are instinctively nurturing. They are nocturnal by nature and like to be awake at night. They are one of the oldest dog breeds. The Great Pyrenees was a war dog that served in both World Wars.

Saint Bernard's are massive dogs that can weigh well over 200 pounds. Even so, they're famously revered as excellent dogs for children. They're one of the few nanny dogs that are dependable, reliable and friendly. They Originate from the French Alps. Saint Bernard's were once used as mountain rescue dogs. Several Saint Bernard's have broken records for their size. They drool a lot.

Boxers need a decent amount of socialization to thrive in a household with kids. Their silly personality and playful nature will be a huge hit with children. In many ways, Boxers are just like goofy kids. Boxers are loyal to the bone, and they make superb guardians. If they sense a threat to the kids, expect them to be there for them. Boxers have a unique undershot jaw. Boxers need to be cleaned regularly. Female Boxers are more hyperactive than males.

Gordon Setters can be a little on the big side. However, the protective and sweet nature of these dogs far outweigh the risk of unintentional injury. They love to be around kids and their caring personalities prove it. The Gordon Setter will do whatever it takes to put a smile on a kids face. Despite their sweet disposition, we advise parental supervision during all play sessions with younger children due to their size. They are the largest of the setter breeds. However, it is one of the slowest breeds to develop. It acts like a pup until the age of three years or more.

Border Collies are energetic and lively dogs. What makes them great for kids is their obedience. Border Collies can learn commands quickly and love to show off. One of the best ways to bond the child-dog relationship is by including the kids in training them. It helps to establish trust and confidence between the two. They respond well to training, even if its with a child. They're one of the smartest dog breeds in the world. One of the quirkiest Guinness world records is held by a Border Collie, who conquered the task of opening a car door window.

The Dalmatian has been a long time favorite of kids all over the world. It's not just because of the movie, 101 dalmatians, but also because of their pleasant temperaments. These dogs are affectionate, energetic, and playful. Dalmatians love to participate in family activities. If you can provide plenty of play time with the dog and kids, they'll be best friends in no time. Dalmatians are born spotless, each Dalmatian has its own unique spots. Fire departments used them as coach dogs.

Keeshonds are good natured dogs with a sweet disposition. They get along great in a household with kids and with other dogs and pets. With their playful nature, these dogs tend to fair well with kids of all ages. The Keeshond can be clingy, they like affection. They are smart and very easy to train. The Keeshond has a long coat and can overheat if left outdoors in the sun.

Cocker Spaniels have a playful energy that can match any child. Cocker Spaniels tend to develop strong bonds with their owners, largely because they're such trusting dogs. While they do love lounging with the adults, they don't mind romping around with children. They are one of the smallest sporting breeds. Cocker Spaniels are one of the first cancer detecting dogs. President Nixon's dog was a Cocker Spaniel.

The Italian Greyhound is a smaller than the greyhound. They get along best with calmer children due to their small size. They are gentle and docile in the home. Despite the size, they make good watch dogs. While Italian Greyhounds are known for their great speed, they would much rather relax than race. They thrive in small spaces and love companionship. Italian Greyhounds pay extra attention to the tone of your voice, and they understand how you are feeling.

Big dogs as large as the Great Dane, can be a hazard for small children. It's not that they're not friendly, but they are big and don't understand their own size and strength. However, they are gentle dogs. It's why so many of them have a reputation of being great nanny dogs. In addition, a Great Dane knows how to be patient around kids. A male Great Dane can weigh 175 pounds. Both males and females can tower over many humans when they stand on their hind legs.

Collies are fluffy yet adorable and kids seem to love them. But they are herding dogs and the lively and bright energy will make them better suited for older kids who like to play. They're gentle dogs in the home. Collies are known to be aloof when it comes to strangers. They are extremely smart dogs. They've broken all kinds of world records. They also make great search and rescue dogs.

The Weimaraner is one of the best companions for older children. Because they're agile and strong, we recommend bringing one home as a puppy. They need to be trained but will thrive once obedience is in check. They have the energy to match even the rowdiest of children, supervision is needed when playing with small children due to their size. They don't have a single aggressive bone in their body. Fantastic for older children. They are deeply devoted to their people. They have an off switch, they know how to relax. They're one of the fastest dog breeds on land.

Cardigan Welsh Corgi is a fan favorite among children all over the world. With their loving nature and cheerful vibe, it's easy to see why. Their energy and enthusiasm are perfect for active kids. Their name means dwarf dog. They have an openness to strangers and want to be best friends with everyone. They have a love for the outdoors, and they thrive on mental stimulation and physical activity.

When people see the Staffordshire Bull Terrier, they tend to think of Pitbull's and scare off. This is a misconception. For those that know these dogs, they're famously touted for their unusual love and affinity with children. However, socializing is crucial, make sure to always supervise interactions and keep a close eye. Other than that, there is a reason why Staffordshire's are trusted by so many families. The Staffordshire is nicknamed the nanny dog, it has the reputation as a child's playmate and guardian. Despite his fierce appearance, this dog is a lover, not a fighter. The breed is gentle, docile, and always on the lookout for fun.

Naturally humorous and playful Pugs make excellent dogs for kids of all ages. They are quiet dogs that won't scare babies, they're gentle companions that understand the fragility of children. Pugs were bred to be lap dogs. They have wrinkles. Pugs are known to have an underbite. Pugs are a low maintenance breed. Pugs only need moderate exercise. Pugs love to sleep.

Puggles get along with kids and other dogs and can make a great family companion. Just be aware that they may enjoy barking, and although they're intelligent and loving, they're not always eager to please when it comes to training. The Puggle is a cross breed, a mix of the Pug and Beagle. Puggles are active and energetic. Puggles shed and need weekly brushing to get rid of loose or dead hair. Puggles are smart, but they can be stubborn.

Due to the high energy levels and activeness of the Vizsla, they're better suited for homes with older kids. The Vizsla can be both active or gentle, depending on the situation. They're intelligent dogs that understand when they should play hard and when they need to relax. To turn them into kid-friendly dogs, socializing is essential. They're highly intelligent. They love affection. They're fast runners. They're born with blue eyes. They lack an insulating undercoat, they get cold easily. They adapt well to small living spaces. They have webbed feet and make good swimmers.

The Munsterlander Pointer is affectionate with family, kids, and other dogs. They excel at water sports and retrieving, if you're not an outdoorsman, you'll need to find other ways to give them physical and mental exercise. The Munsterlander is best suited in a working home where he can use his skills as a hunting dog. He is affectionate and loves attention, this makes him a great family companion. Like all sporting dogs, though, he is high energy and requires a lot of exercise to keep from getting bored. He can run for hours so be sure to provide ample opportunity for him to run.

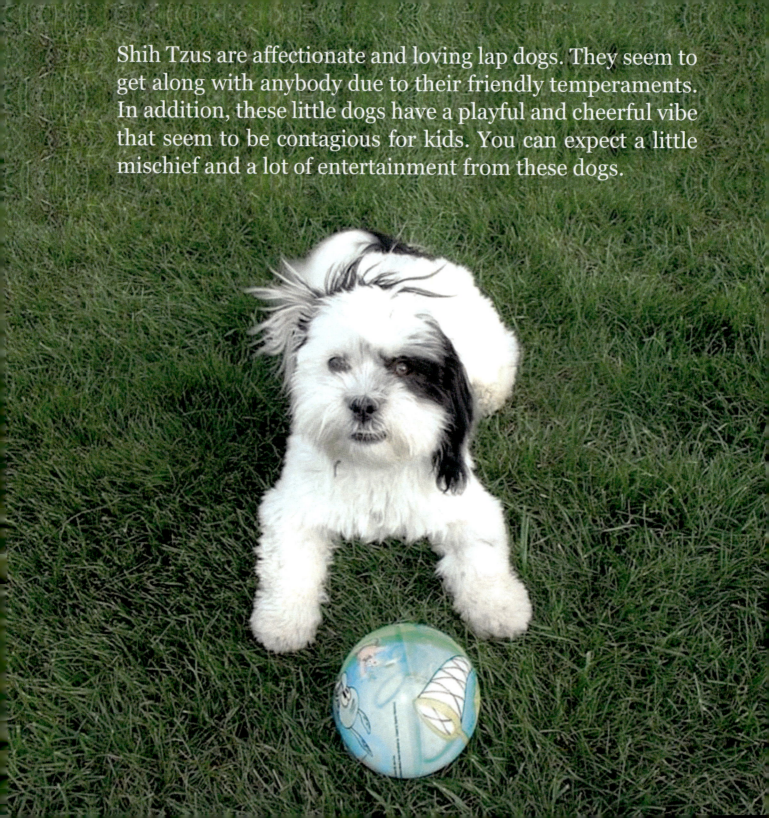

Shih Tzus are affectionate and loving lap dogs. They seem to get along with anybody due to their friendly temperaments. In addition, these little dogs have a playful and cheerful vibe that seem to be contagious for kids. You can expect a little mischief and a lot of entertainment from these dogs.

The English setter is a gentle, friendly dog that is especially good with children. They are mild mannered and sensitive and love to both give and receive affection. An English setter requires exercise, they are highly active dogs. English Setters are sporting dogs. They're good for first time dog owners. English Setters are a rare dog breed. English Setter puppies require toys to play with.

The End

Thanks for taking time to read our book.

To Check Out More of Our Books

Visit

Billy Grinslott or Kinsey Marie Books

Author Page

Billy Grinslott & Kinsey Marie Books

Copyright, All Rights Reserved.

ISBN - 9781957881959

Made in the USA
Middletown, DE
17 March 2024